EDGE
BOOKS

DIRT BIKES

Enduro Racing

by Nick Healy

Consultant:

Alex Edge
Associate Editor
MotorcycleDaily.com

Capstone
press

Mankato, Minnesota

Edge Books are published by Capstone Press,
151 Good Counsel Drive, P.O. Box 669, Mankato, Minnesota 56002.
www.capstonepress.com

Library of Congress Cataloging-in-Publication Data
Healy, Nick.
    Enduro racing / by Nick Healy.
    p. cm.—(Edge books. Dirt bikes)
    Summary: "Describes the sport of enduro racing, the types of motorcycles used, major
competitions, and athletes involved"—Provided by publisher.
    Includes bibliographical references and index.
    ISBN 0-7368-4364-7 (hardcover)
1. Motocross—Juvenile literature. I. Title. II. Series.
GV1060.12.H43 2006
796.7'56—dc22   2005005814

Editorial Credits
Connie Colwell Miller, editor; Jason Knudson, set designer; Kate Opseth,
    book designer; Wanda Winch, photo researcher; Scott Thoms, photo editor

Photo Credits
Getty Images Inc./Francois Dubourg, 29
Idario Araujo, 14
Mark Kariya, cover, 5, 7, 8, 11, 13, 17, 18, 20, 27, 28
Photo courtesy Motorcycle Hall of Fame Museum, 24
Top Speed Productions/Michael Demaree, 23

1 2 3 4 5 6 10 09 08 07 06 05

Table of Contents

CHAPTER 1

Enduro Racing

A rider bounces along a narrow trail on a motorcycle. Mud flies from the motorcycle's tires. It coats both the machine and the rider. His shoulders almost touch the trees that line the route.

No fans cheer the rider on. No other riders race against him. The rider is racing against the clock. The rider climbs steep slopes and races down hillsides. He faces thick woods, swampy clearings, and rocky gullies.

Learn about:
- Endurance run
- Race timing
- Enduro courses

Enduro riders usually come off the course covered in mud.

The rider glances at the small computer attached to his handlebars. He spots a route marker on a tree. The course takes a sharp turn. The rider grips the brakes, takes the corner, and speeds onward.

Enduro Basics

Motorcycle enduros are unlike other motorcycle races. Riders usually don't race against other people at the same time.

Enduros are about endurance. The sport's name comes from "endurance run." Enduros test the strength of riders and their motorcycles. Riders follow a marked course through the countryside. They stop at checkpoints along the way. They are scored for their ability to ride the course in a set amount of time.

Markers posted on trees show riders how to follow enduro courses.

Enduro riders travel on everything from mud to sand.

Enduro courses are carefully planned. They are marked with flags and signs. These markers tell the riders where to turn and help keep riders from getting lost.

Enduro courses wind along for miles. Courses differ in total distance. Many enduro courses are 40 to 100 miles (64 to 160 kilometers) long. Some enduros run as long as 500 miles (800 kilometers) and take place over two days.

Every enduro course features rough terrain. Riders encounter mud and rocks, woods and mountains, and hills and valleys. They ride on old logging roads, cow paths, and overgrown trails. They never know what obstacles will be around the next turn.

CHAPTER 2

Rules of the Sport

Skill is more important than speed in motorcycle enduros. Riders do not compete to be the first across the finish line. Instead, they try to get a better score than other competitors. In enduro, the best score is zero.

Race scoring is simple. Riders get points for each minute early or late they reach a checkpoint. Riders who make it right on time get no points. The winner is the rider who finishes with the fewest points.

Learn about:

- Scoring
- Championships
- ISDE

In enduro racing, skill is more important than speeding to the finish line.

Checkpoints

Enduro courses include checkpoints. Riders are expected to reach each of these locations at a certain time. They should not travel too fast or too slow.

Before the race, all riders receive a route sheet. The sheet tells them the distance between checkpoints. The route sheet also tells riders the speed they should travel.

There are also secret or emergency checkpoints. These checkpoints do not appear on the route sheet. Riders' times are recorded at these checkpoints too.

Enduro Championships

Thousands of riders compete in motorcycle enduros each year. They ride in amateur and pro races. Hundreds of events take place around the world.

Top riders battle for national and world championships. In the United States, pro riders compete for the American Motorcyclist Association (AMA) National Enduro Championship title. The AMA sanctions, or approves, a series of races each year. Racers receive points for placing high in sanctioned races. The rider with the most points at the end of the series wins the championship.

Riders must travel at an exact speed so they arrive at checkpoints at a certain time.

The ISDE takes place in countries around the world.

Pro riders from around the world compete at the World Enduro Championship. They race in events sanctioned by the Federation of International Motorcyclists.

ISDE

The International Six Days' Enduro (ISDE) began in England in 1913. No other enduro event is like it.

Nations around the world send teams to compete in the event. For the first five days, riders complete two courses of about 85 miles (136 kilometers). On the final day, riders complete a shorter course.

CHAPTER 3

Equipment and Safety

Enduro riders try to be safe and finish on time. To do so, they rely on their equipment. Many riders attach small computers to their handlebars. The computers tell riders their speed and how far they have traveled. They also let riders know whether they must speed up or slow down to finish on time.

Learn about:

- Equipment
- Enduro bikes
- Safety gear

Enduro riders wear special gear to keep them safe as they ride.

To be lightweight, enduro bikes have few extra parts.

Dirt Bikes

Enduro racers ride on dirt bikes. These motorcycles are made for off-road riding. The bikes' frames are high off the ground. The bikes can clear bumps or other obstacles. Riders sit about 36 inches (91 centimeters) off the ground.

Riders want their bikes to be lightweight. They strip off all parts they don't need. For example, enduro bikes do not have kickstands. Top riders use bikes weighing only about 240 pounds (108 kilograms). Other motocross bikes can weigh as much as 500 pounds (227 kilograms).

Enduro riders need some features on their bikes that other motocross racers do not. They need headlights, taillights, and a speedometer. These items make travel on enduro courses easier.

Racers use motorcycles from several different companies. The most popular dirt bike companies are Yamaha, Kawasaki, KTM, Suzuki, Honda, and Hasqvarna.

Body armor helps prevent injuries to riders in case of a crash.

Safety

Riders must have equipment to keep comfortable and safe. They wear lightweight clothing to stay cool during races. They wear helmets, goggles, gloves, and tall boots for protection. Padding covers their knees, elbows, and shoulders to prevent injuries in crashes. Riders also wear plastic body armor to prevent injuries.

Safety gear helps riders, but skill and fitness are also important. Riders work out to keep themselves in good shape. They need energy to handle their bikes, so good nutrition is important. They must be quick and calm in any weather conditions. The best riders can handle any demand nature provides.

CHAPTER 4

Enduro Stars

Top American enduro racers are honored in the AMA's Motorcycle Hall of Fame and Museum. The museum is located near Columbus, Ohio. Each year, more motorcycle legends are voted into the Hall.

Bill Baird is one of a handful of enduro riders in the Hall of Fame. In 1962, Baird won his first AMA National Enduro Championship. He won again the next year. He kept on winning for seven straight years.

Learn about:
- Enduro legends
- Stars of today
- The world's best

Today, more riders want to become enduro stars.

Bill Baird was an enduro star of the 1960s.

Only one rider has beaten Baird's record. Starting in 1974, Richard Burleson won eight straight National Enduro Championships. His winning streak earned him the nickname "King Richard."

Many enduro champions learn to ride at a young age. But Burleson did not ride a motorcycle until he was 18. Burleson decided to try enduro in college, and he learned he was skilled at the sport.

Today's Top Riders

Mike "Junior" Lafferty is one of the top riders in North America. Lafferty is from New Jersey. He first won the National Enduro Championship in 1997. In 2003, he won his sixth championship. It was his fourth in a row.

In 2004, Lafferty injured his knee. He could not ride for four months. He returned for a major event in northern Michigan. Lafferty won the enduro by two points.

Randy Hawkins is another top rider. He is from South Carolina and has run enduros for nearly 20 years. He won six National Enduro Championships between 1988 and 1996. Hawkins finished second to Lafferty in 2002 and 2003.

The World's Best

The World Enduro Championship series also features stars. Kari Tiainen and Juha Salminen are from Finland. Tiainen won seven World Enduro titles from 1990 to 2000. Salminen won the first of five straight titles in 1999. Both were members of Finnish teams that won the ISDE.

Randy Hawkins is one of today's top enduro riders.

Finnish rider Kari Tiainen has been a world enduro champ seven times.

Swedish rider Anders Eriksson is another of World Enduro's best. Eriksson has won seven World Enduro titles. He rode with the Swedish team that won the 1992 Junior Trophy at the ISDE. He won his first championship in 1995. Since then, he has won seven world championships.

Enduro racing is quickly becoming a popular sport. New fans and racers continue to become more interested in enduro. Fans keep watching for new stars in this exciting sport.

The sport of enduro racing continues to gain popularity.

Glossary

amateur (AM-uh-chur)—a competitor who does not earn money for competing in a sport

endurance (en-DUR-uhns)—the ability to keep doing an activity for a long period of time

obstacle (OB-stuh-kuhl)—something that gets in the way or prevents someone from doing something

sanction (SANGK-shun)—to officially approve or support

terrain (tuh-RAYN)—land or ground

Read More

Freeman, Gary. *Motocross.* To the Limit. Austin, Texas: Raintree Steck-Vaughn, 2001.

Hendrickson, Steve. *Enduro Racing.* Motorcycles. Mankato, Minn.: Capstone Press, 2000.

Kalman, Bobbie, and John Crossingham. *Extreme Motocross.* Extreme Sports No Limits! New York: Crabtree Publishing, 2004.

Internet Sites

FactHound offers a safe, fun way to find Internet sites related to this book. All of the sites on FactHound have been researched by our staff.

Here's how:

1. Visit *www.facthound.com*
2. Type in this special code **0736843647** for age-appropriate sites. Or enter a search word related to this book for a more general search.
3. Click on the **Fetch It** button.

FactHound will fetch the best sites for you!

Index